The Best Of BOB DYLAN

HAL•LEONARD®

Exclusive Distributors:

Hal Leonard Europe Limited
42 Wigmore Street
Marylebone, London, W1U 2RN, UK
Email: info@halleonardeurope.com

Hal Leonard
7777 West Bluemound Road
Milwaukee, WI 53213, USA
Email: info@halleonard.com

Hal Leonard Australia Pty. Ltd.
4 Lentara Court
Cheltenham, Victoria, 3192, Australia
Email: info@halleonard.com.au

Order No. AM955060
ISBN 978-0-7119-7003-8
This book © Copyright 1997 by Hal Leonard.

Printed in the EU.

Blowin' In The Wind 4
The Times They Are A-Changin' 10
Don't Think Twice, It's All Right 12
Mr Tambourine Man 7
Like A Rolling Stone 16
Just Like A Woman 20
All Along The Watchtower 24
Lay Lady Lay 28
I Shall Be Released 33
If Not For You 36
Knockin' On Heaven's Door 42
Forever Young 44
Tangled Up In Blue 50
Oh, Sister 47
Gotta Serve Somebody 54
Jokerman 58
Everything Is Broken 62
Shelter From The Storm 68

Blowin' In The Wind

Words & Music by Bob Dylan.

seas must a white dove ___ sail be - fore she
ears ___ must one - man ___ have be - fore he can

sleeps in the sand? Yes, 'n' how man - y
hear peo - ple cry? Yes, 'n' how man - y

times must the can - non - balls fly be - fore they're
deaths will it take 'til he knows d and that too man - y

for - ev - er banned?
peo - ple have died? } The an - swer, my

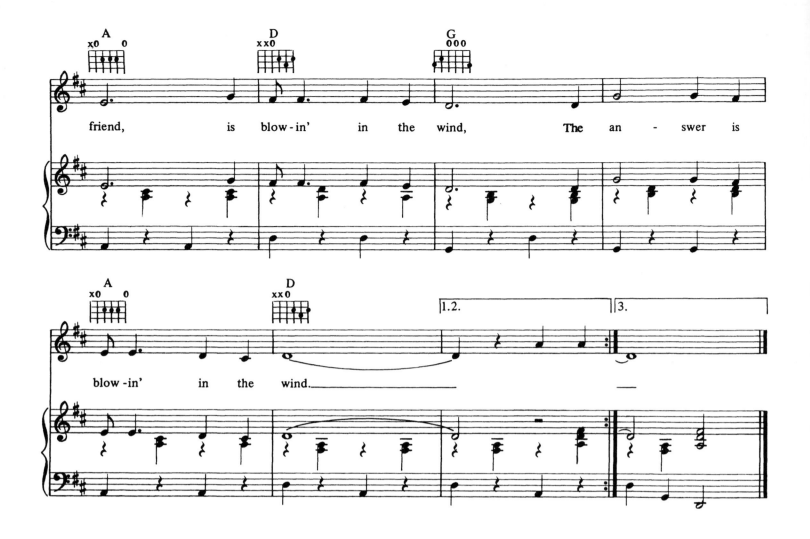

friend, is blow-in' in the wind, The an - swer is

blow-in' in the wind.

Additional Lyrics

3. How many years can a mountain exist
   before it is washed to the sea?
   Yes 'n' how many years can some people exist
   before they're allowed to be free?
   Yes 'n' how many times can a man turn his head
   pretending that he just doesn't see?

   The answer, my friend, is blowin' in the wind,
   The answer is blowin' in the wind.

Mr Tambourine Man

Words & Music by Bob Dylan.

fifth time Fine

jin - gle jan - gle morn-in' I'll come fol - low-in' you.

Verse

1. Thought I know that eve - nin's em - pire has re-turned in - to sand,

Van-ished from my hand, left me blind - ly here to stand but still not

sleep-in'! My wea - ri - ness a - maz - es me I'm

brand - ed on my feet. I have no one to meet and the

Repeat three times

an - cient emp - ty street's too dead for dream in'. _____

Refrain:

Verse 2. Take me on a trip upon your magic swirlin' ship
My senses have been stripped, my hands can't feel to grip
My toes too numb to step, wait only for my boot heels
To be wanderin'
I'm ready to go anywhere, I'm ready for to fade
Into my own parade, cast your dancin' spell my way
I promise to go under it.

Refrain:

Verse 3. Though you might hear laughin' spinnin' swingin' madly across the sun
It's not aimed at anyone, it's just escapin' on the run
And but for the sky there are no fences facin'
And if you hear vague traces of skippin' reels of rhyme
To your tambourine in time, it's just a ragged clown behind
I wouldn't pay it any mind, it's just a shadow you're
Seein' that he's chasin'.

Refrain:

Verse 4. Then take me disappearin' through the smoke rings of my mind
Down the foggy ruins of time, far past the frozen leaves
The haunted, frightened trees out to the windy beach
Far from the twisted reach of crazy sorrow
Yes, to dance beneath the diamond sky with one hand wavin' free
Silhouetted by the sea, circled by the circus sands
With all memory and fate driven deep beneath the waves
Let me forget about today until tomorrow.

Refrain:

The Times They Are A-Changin'

Words & Music by Bob Dylan.

Moderately

1. Come gath-er 'round peo-ple where-ev-er you roam _____ And ad-
2.-5. *See additional lyrics*

mit that the wa-ters a-round you have grown And ac-cept it that

soon you'll be drenched to the bone. _____ If your time to you is worth

Additional lyrics

2. Come writers and critics who prophecize with your pen
And keep your eyes wide the chance won't come again
And don't speak too soon for the wheel's still in spin
And there's no tellin' who that it's namin'.
For the loser now will be later to win
For the times they are a-changin'.

3. Come senators, congressmen please heed the call
Don't stand in the doorway don't block the hall
For he that gets hurt will be he who has stalled
There's a battle outside and it's ragin'.
It'll soon shake your windows and rattle your walls
For the times they are a-changin'.

4. Come mothers and fathers throughout the land
And don't criticize what you can't understand
Your sons and your daughters are beyond your command
Your old road is rapidly agin'.
Please get out of the new one if you can't lend your hand
For the times they are a-changin'.

5. The line it is drawn the curse it is cast
The slow one now will later be fast
As the present now will later be past
The order is rapidly fadin'.
And the first one now will later be last
For the times they are a-changin'.

Don't Think Twice, It's All Right

Words & Music by Bob Dylan.

Moderato

now.
road.
When the roost - er crows at the break of
Still I wish there was some-thin' you would do or

dawn
say
Look out your win - dow and _____ I'll be gone.
To try and make me change my ___ mind and stay.

You're the rea - son I'm trav'-lin' on
We nev - er did too ___ much talk - in' an-y - way

Don't think
So don't think

twice, it's all right.
2. It right.
3. I'm
(4. It)

Like A Rolling Stone

Words & Music by Bob Dylan.

scroung - ing   for your next   meal. _____

chorus

How does it feel   How does it feel

To be with-out a home

Like a com-plete un-known   like a roll-ing stone?

18

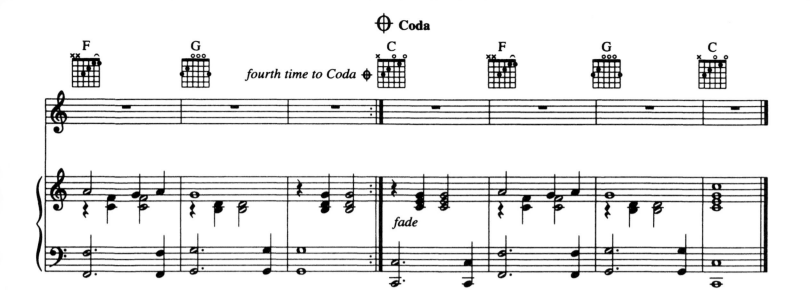

Additional lyrics

2. You've gone to the finest school all right Miss Lonely
   But you know you only used to get juiced in it
   And nobody's every taught you how to live on the street
   And now find out you're gonna have to get used to it
   You said you'd never compromise
   With the mystery tramp, but now you realize
   He's not selling any alibis
   As you stare into the vacuum of his eyes
   And ask him do you want to make a deal?
   Chorus

3. You never turned around to see the frowns on the jugglers and the clowns
   When they all come down and did tricks for you
   You never understood that it ain't no good
   You shouldn't let other people get your kicks for you
   You used to ride on the chrome horse with your diplomat
   Who carried on his shoulder a Siamese cat
   Ain't it hard when you discovered that
   He really wasn't where it's at
   After he took from you everything he could steal.
   Chorus

4. Princess on the steeple and all the pretty people
   They're drinkin', thinkin' that they got it made
   Exchanging all kinds of precious gifts and things
   But you'd better lift your diamond ring, you'd better pawn it babe
   You used to be so amused
   At Napoleon in rags and the language that he used
   Go to him now, he calls you, you can't refuse
   When you got nothing, you got nothing to lose
   You're invisible now, you got no secrets to conceal.
   Chorus

Just Like A Woman

Words & Music by Bob Dylan.

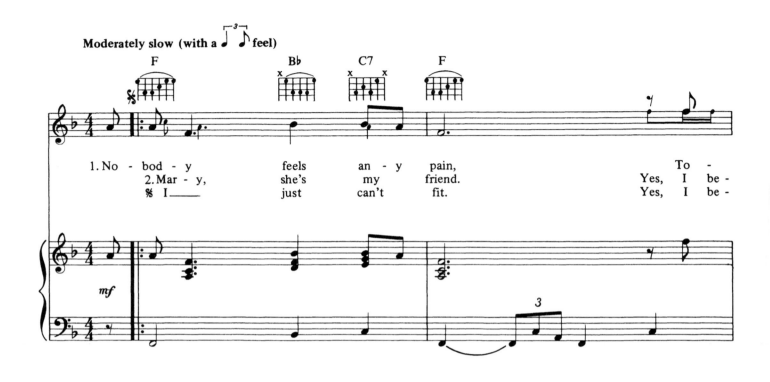

1. No - bod - y feels an - y pain, To -
2. Mar - y, she's my friend. Yes, I be -
§ I just can't fit. Yes, I be -

night as I stand in - side the rain, Ev - 'ry - bod - y knows that
lieve I'll go see her a - gain. No - bod - y has to guess that
lieve it's time for us to quit. When we meet a - gain,

ba - by's got new clothes. But late - ly, I see her
ba - by can't be blessed Till she sees fi - nal - ly that
in - tro - duced as friends, Please don't let on

rib - bons and her bows have fall - en from her
she's like all the rest with her fog, her am-phet-a - mine, and her
that you knew me when I was hun - gry and it was your

curls. She takes just like a wom - an, yes, she does. She
pearls. She takes just like a wom - an, yes, she does. She
world. Ah, you fake just like a wom - an, yes, you do. You

All Along The Watchtower

Words & Music by Bob Dylan.

drink my wine.__ Plow - men__ dig my earth, None of them a -

long the line_____ know what an - y of it is worth."__

"No rea - son to get ex - cit - ed," the thief, he kind - ly spoke, __

"There are man - y here a - mong us

Prin - ces kept the view,__ While all the wom-en came and went,

Bare - foot ser - vants, too. __ Out - side__ in the dis - tance,

A wild - cat did growl,__ Two rid - ers were ap -

proach - ing, The wind be - gan to howl.

27

Lay Lady Lay

Words & Music by Bob Dylan.

His clothes are dirt - y but his___ hands are clean,___

And you're the best___ thing that he's ev - er seen.___

Stay, la - dy, stay,___ stay with your man___ a - while.

Why wait an - y long - er for___ the world to be - gin,___

stay while the night __ is still a - head. __

I long __ to see __ you in the morn - ing light, __ I long to reach __ for you

in the night. __ Stay, la - dy, stay, __ stay while the night __ is still a - head. __

32

I Shall Be Released

Words & Music by Bob Dylan.

Additional Lyrics

2. Down here next to me in this lonely crowd
   Is a man who swears he's not to blame.
   All day long I hear him cry so loud,
   Calling out that he's been framed.

   Chorus

3. They say ev'rything can be replaced,
   Yet ev'ry distance is not near.
   So I remember ev'ry face
   Of ev'ry man who put me here.

   Chorus

If Not For You

Words & Music by Bob Dylan.

If not for you.

If not for you,_

Babe, I'd_ lay a-wake all night,_ Wait for the

morn - in' light_ to shine in through,_

be lost, if not for you, And you know it's true.

If not for you, My sky would fall,

Rain would gath-er too. ___ With-out your love, I'd

be no-where at all. Oh! ___ What would I ___ do, ___ If not ___ for you. ___

If not for you, ___

Win-ter would

Knockin' On Heaven's Door

Words & Music by Bob Dylan.

I feel like I'm knock-in' on heav-en's door.__
I feel like I'm knock-in' on heav-en's door.__

Knock, knock, knock-in' on heav-en's door,___

Knock, knock, knock-in' on heav-en's door,___

Knock, knock, knock-in' on heav-en's door,___

Knock, knock, knock-in' on heav-en's door.___

Repeat and fade

Forever Young

Words & Music by Bob Dylan.

Moderately slow, with a steady beat

1.May God bless and keep you al - ways,__ May your wish - es all come true. May you

al - ways do for oth - ers, And let oth - ers do for you.__ May you

build a lad - der to the stars and climb on ev -'ry rung.__ May you

stay   for - ev - er young,   May you

stay_____ for - ev - er young.   2. May you

grow up to be right - eous,   May you grow up to be   true.___   May you
hands al - ways be bus - y,   May your feet al - ways be swift.___   May you

al - ways   know the truth,___   And see the lights sur - round - ing you.   May you
have a   strong foun-da - tion   when the winds of chang - es shift.   May your

al - ways be cou - ra - geous, **Stand** up - right and be strong._ May you
heart **al** - ways be joy - ful, May your song al - ways be sung._ May you

stay for - ev - er young, May you

stay_____ for - ev - er young. 3. May you stay_____ for - ev - er

young, May you stay_____ for - ev - er young.

Oh, Sister

Music by Bob Dylan. Words by Bob Dylan & Jacques Levy.

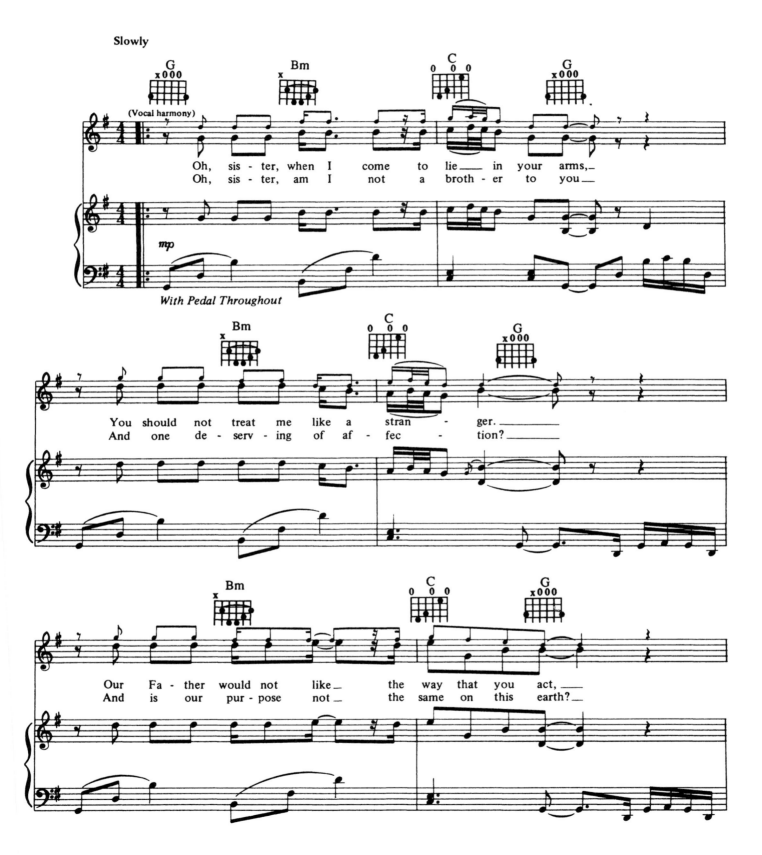

And you must re-al-ize The dan - ger.
To love and fol-low His di - rec - tion.

We grew up to-geth-er from the cra-dle to the grave.___ We

died and were re-born and then Mys-te-ri-ous-ly saved.___ Oh, sis-ter, when I come to

knock on your door,_ Don't turn a-way, you'll cre-ate sor-row._

Time is an o-cean but it ends at the shore._ You may not see me To-mor-row.

Tangled Up In Blue

Words & Music by Bob Dylan.

Moderately, in 2

1. Ear - ly one morn - in' the sun was shin - in', I was lay - in' in bed,___

___ Won - d'rin' if___ she'd changed at all,___ If her hair___ was still

51

2. She was married when we first met,
   Soon to be divorced.
   I helped her out of a jam, I guess,
   But I used a little too much force.
   We drove that car as far as we could,
   Abandoned it out West.
   Split up on a dark sad night,
   Both agreeing it was best.
   She turned around to look at me,
   As I was walkin' away.
   I heard her say over my shoulder,
   "We'll meet again some day
   on the avenue."
   Tangled up in blue.

3. I had a job in the great north woods,
   Working as a cook for a spell.
   But I never did like it all that much,
   And one day the axe just fell.
   So I drifted down to New Orleans,
   Where I happened to be employed.
   Workin' for a while on a fishin' boat,
   Right outside of Delacroix.
   But all the while I was alone,
   The past was close behind.
   I seen a lot of women,
   But she never escaped my mind,
   And I just grew.
   Tangled up in blue.

4. She was workin' in a topless place,
   And I stopped in for a beer.
   I just kept lookin' at the side of her face,
   In the spotlight so clear.
   And later on as the crowd thinned out,
   I's just about to do the same.
   She was standing there in back of my chair,
   Said to me, "Don't I know your name?"
   I muttered somethin' underneath my breath,
   She studied the lines on my face.
   I must admit I felt a little uneasy,
   When she bent down to tie the laces
   Of my shoe.
   Tangled up in blue.

5. She lit a burner on the stove,
   And offered me a pipe.
   "I thought you'd never say hello," she said,
   "You look like the silent type."
   Then she opened up a book of poems,
   And handed it to me.
   Written by an Italian poet
   From the thirteenth century.
   And every one of them words rang true,
   And glowed like burnin' coal.
   Pourin' off of every page,
   Like it was written in my soul
   From me to you.
   Tangled up in blue.

6. I lived with them on Montague Street,
   In a basement down the stairs.
   There was music in the cafes at night,
   And revolution in the air.
   Then he started into dealing with slaves,
   And something inside of him died.
   She had to sell everything she owned,
   And froze up inside.
   And when finally the bottom fell out,
   I became withdrawn.
   The only thing I knew how to do,
   Was to keep on keepin' on,
   Like a bird that flew.
   Tangled up in blue.

7. So now I'm goin' back again,
   I got to get to her somehow.
   All the people we used to know,
   They're an illusion to me now.
   Some are mathematicians,
   Some are carpenters' wives.
   Don't know how it all got started,
   I don't know what they're doin' with their lives.
   But me, I'm still on the road,
   Headin' for another joint.
   We always did feel the same,
   We just saw it from a different point
   Of view.
   Tangled up in blue.

Gotta Serve Somebody

Words & Music by Bob Dylan.

Moderately slow

sempre simile

Verse:

1. You may be an am-bas-sa-dor_ to Eng-land or France._

You may like to gam-ble, you might like to dance._

You may_ be the heav - y - weight_ cham - pion of the world._

Chorus:

You may be a so - cial - ite_ with a long_____ string of pearls. But you're gon - na have to

D7

serve some - bod - y,   yes in - deed.___ You're gon - na have to serve___

Am

___ some - bod - y.   Well,

it may be the dev - il or___ it___ may be the Lord. But you're gon - na have to

serve some - bod - y.

2. You

2. You might be a rock'n'roll addict prancing on the stage.
   You might have drugs at your command, women in a cage.
   You may be a businessman or some high degree thief.
   They may call you doctor, or they may call you chief.
   Chorus

3. You may be a state trooper, you might be a young Turk.
   You might be the head of some big TV network.
   You may be rich or poor, you may be blind or lame.
   You may be leaving in another country under another name.
   Chorus

4. You may be a construction worker working on a home.
   You may be living in a mansion, or you might live in a dome.
   You might own guns and you might even own tanks.
   You might be somebody's landlord, you might even own banks.
   Chorus

5. You may be a preacher with your spiritual pride.
   You may be a city councilman taking bribes on the side.
   You may be workin' in a barbershop, you may know how to cut hair.
   You may be somebody's mistress, may be somebody's heir.
   Chorus

6. Might like to wear cotton, might like to wear silk.
   Might like to drink whiskey, might like to drink milk.
   You might like to eat caviar, you might like to eat bread.
   You may be sleeping on the floor, sleeping in a king-sized bed.
   Chorus

7. You may call me Terry, you may call me Timmy.
   You may call me Bobby, you may call me Zimmy.
   You may call me R.J., you may call me Ray.
   You may call me anything, but no matter what you say.
   Chorus

Jokerman

Words & Music by Bob Dylan.

2. So swiftly the sun sets in the sky.
   You rise up and say goodbye to no one.
   Fools rush in where angels fear to tread.
   Both of their futures, so full of dread, you don't show one.
   Shedding off one more layer of skin,
   Keeping one step ahead of the persecutor within.
   Chorus

3. You're a man of the mountains, you can walk on the clouds.
   Manipulator of crowds, you're a dream twister.
   You're going to Sodom and Gomorrah,
   But what do you care? Ain't nobody there would want to marry your sister.
   Friend to the martyr, a friend to the woman of shame,
   You look into the fiery furnace, see the rich man without any name.
   Chorus

4. Well, the Book of Leviticus and Deuteronomy,
   The law of the jungle and the sea are your only teachers.
   In the smoke of the twilight on a milk-white steed,
   Michelangelo indeed could've carved out your features.
   Resting in the fields, far from the turbulent space,
   Half asleep near the stars with a small dog licking your face.
   Chorus

5. Well, the rifleman's stalking the sick and the lame,
   Preacherman seeks the same, who'll get there first is uncertain.
   Nightsticks and water cannons, teargas, padlocks,
   Molotov cocktails and rocks behind every curtain.
   Falsehearted judges dying in the webs that they spin,
   Only a matter of time till night comes steppin' in.
   Chorus

6. It's a shadowy world, skies are slippery grey.
   A woman just gave birth to a prince today and dressed him in scarlet.
   He'll put the priest in his pocket, put the blade to the heat,
   Take the motherless children off the street,
   And place them at the feet of a harlot.
   Oh, Jokerman, you know what he wants,
   Oh, Jokerman, you don't show any response.
   Chorus

Everything Is Broken

Words & Music by Bob Dylan.

Moderately, with a steady beat

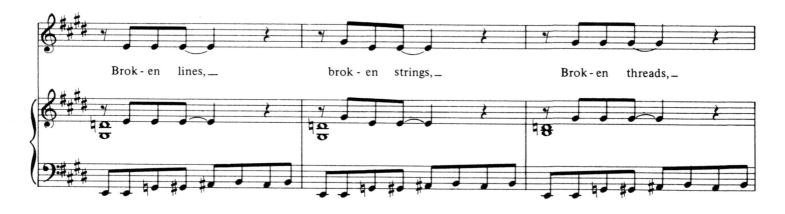

Brok-en lines,＿ brok-en strings,＿ Brok-en threads,＿

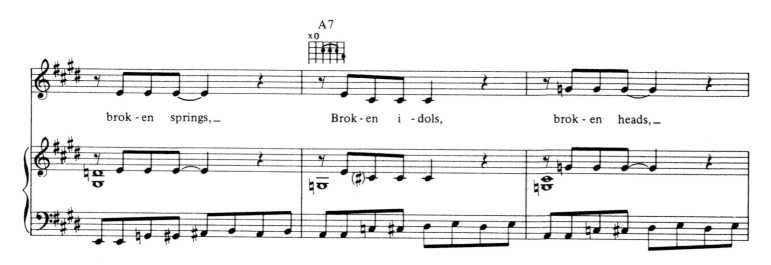

brok-en springs,＿ Brok-en i-dols, brok-en heads,＿

Seem like ev - ery time you stop and

turn a - round, ___ Some - thing else ___ just hit the ground. ___

Brok - en cut - ters, brok - en saws, ___ Brok - en buck - les,

brok - en laws, ___ Brok - en bod - ies, brok - en bones, ___

Shelter From The Storm

Words & Music by Bob Dylan.

Moderately, in 2

1. 'Twas in an - oth - er life - time, one of toil and blood,____
word was spoke be - tween__ us, there was lit - tle risk in - volved;____
ly I turned a - round__ and she was stand - in' there____
dep - u - ty walks on hard__ nails and the preach - er rides a mount;____
lit - tle hill - top vil - age they gam - bled for my clothes;____

when black - ness was a vir - tue and the
ev - 'ry - thing up to__ that point had been
with sil - ver brace - lets on__ her wrists and
but noth - ing real - ly mat - ters much, it's
I bar - gained for sal - va - tion an' they

road was full of mud.____ I came in from' the wil -
left un - re - solved.____ Try im ag - in - ing a place -
flow - ers in her hair.____ She walked up to me so grace -
doom a lone that counts.____ And the one-eyed un - der - tak -
gave me a le - thal dose.____ I of - fered up____ my in -

der - ness, a crea - ture void of form,____
____ where it's al - ways safe and warm,____
ful - ly and took my crown of thorns,____
er, he blows a fu - tile horn,____ "Come
no - cence and got re - paid with scorn,____

in," she said, "I'll give you shel - ter from_ the storm."

In a world of steel-eyed death and men who are
Hunt-ed like a croc-o-dile,
Just to think that it all be-gan on a
Do I un-der-stand your ques-tion, man, is it
If I could on-ly turn back the clock to when

fight-ing to be warm.
rav-aged in the corn,
long for-got-ten morn,
hope-less and for-lorn?
God and her were born,

"Come in," she said, "I'll give

you shel-ter from the storm."

2. Not a
3. Sud-den-
4. Well, the
5. In a

ritard.

Bringing you the words and the music

All the latest music in print... rock & pop plus jazz, blues, country, classical and the best in West End show scores.

- Books to match your favourite CDs.

- Book-and-CD titles with high quality backing tracks for you to play along to. Now you can play guitar or piano with your favourite artist... or simply sing along!

- Audition songbooks with CD backing tracks for both male and female singers for all those with stars in their eyes.

- Can't read music? No problem, you can still play all the hits with our wide range of chord songbooks.

- Check out our range of instrumental tutorial titles, taking you from novice to expert in no time at all!

- Musical show scores include *The Phantom Of The Opera*, *Les Misérables*, *Mamma Mia* and many more hit productions.

- DVD master classes featuring the techniques of top artists.

EXCLUSIVELY DISTRIBUTED BY

HAL•LEONARD®